Korka was a very small elf.
He was smaller than all the other elves
on Elf Hill.

Korka always wanted to help the big elves.
"You are too small to help us," said one of
the big elves. "Just go home."

Read pages 4 to 6

Purpose: To find out what happened while Korka was in his bed dreaming.

Pause at page 6

Who came to Elf Hill? What did he do?
Where was Korka and what was he doing?

Why are there two words in bold on page 4?
Let's read this sentence together, and make the words sound loud and scary.

Tricky word (page 5):
The word 'knight' may be beyond the children's word recognition skills. Tell this word to the children and explain that the 'k' is silent.

4

That night a **big, bad** troll came to Elf Hill.
The troll jumped on the elf houses
and squashed them.
The elves ran away into the wood.

Korka was in bed, asleep.
He was dreaming.
In his dream, he was
Korka the Mighty Knight,
saving his people from fright.

Suddenly Korka heard a **loud** crash.
He opened his eyes and saw a big troll foot.
Korka's bed was stuck on the troll's foot.

READ

Read pages 7 to 9

Purpose: To find out what happens to Korka and what the troll tells the other trolls.

EXPLORE

Pause at page 9

What happened to Korka? Why didn't the troll see Korka?

Where are they? What does the first troll say to the other trolls? What do the other trolls want to do?

Then the troll ran back to his cave.
Korka jumped off the troll's foot.
"I'm glad the troll didn't see me,"
said Korka.

When the troll got back to the troll cave,
he boasted to the other trolls.
"I jumped on the elf houses and
I squashed them," he laughed.

"We want to do it, too!" said all the trolls.
Korka was hiding in the cave.
He heard what the trolls said.
"Oh, no!" said Korka. "I must stop the trolls."

READ

Read pages 10 and 11

Purpose: To find out what Korka's idea was.

EXPLORE

Pause at page 11

What is Korka doing?

Do you think the stew will taste good? Why do you think Korka put soap in a stew?

Tricky word (page 10):
The word 'idea' may be beyond the children's word recognition skills. Tell this word to the children.

Korka didn't know what to do.
Then he had an idea.
When the trolls were not looking,
he took some soap and a long pipe.

Korka put the soap into the trolls' stew.
It made lots of bubbles.

Read pages 12 and 13

READ

Purpose: To find out if Korka's trick worked or not.

Pause at page 13

EXPLORE

Why are the trolls holding their stomachs?

What words describe the noises they made?
(*moaned, groaned*)

The trolls ate the stew.
It made them feel sick.
They **moaned** and they **groaned**,
and they had to lie down.

Read pages 14 and 15

READ

Purpose: To find out how Korka scared the trolls away.

Pause at page 15

EXPLORE

Korka played two tricks on the trolls. What were they?

What did the trolls do? Why were they scared?

Can you read the words Korka says in a scary voice?

What two words describe the noises the trolls made? (*screamed, squealed*)

Korka stood in front of the fire.
His shadow was very tall.
Then he took the pipe and said,
"I am Korka the Mighty Elf."

Korka's voice was very LOUD.
The trolls were very scared.
They screamed and they squealed,
and they all ran away.

READ

Read the last page

Purpose: To find out how the elves felt towards
Korka now.

EXPLORE

Pause at page 16

How have the other elves' feelings changed?

How do you think Korka felt?

Can you read the words the elves said in the way they
might have said them?

After Reading
Revisit and Respond

- Ask the children in groups to read the story aloud (with each child reading a section), with pace and expression appropriate to the type style and grammar.

- Ask the children to discuss the theme of the story (the triumph of brain over brawn). Can they name any other stories with a similar theme (e.g. *The Hare and the Tortoise, The Clever Chick*).

- Ask the children to describe how Korka felt at the different stages of the story – at the beginning, in the trolls' cave, when he thought up his plan, and when back home with the elves.

- Ask the children to list examples where the text is presented differently (i.e. bold, italic, enlarged), and for each example, describe how it should be read.

- Ask them to look at pages 8, 10 and 13 to find words in the story with the long phoneme 'oa' (*boasted, soap, moaned, groaned*). Then ask them to brainstorm a list.

- Ask them in groups to read through the book again and make a list of things that they wouldn't believe in real life (*e.g. elves living on a hill, trolls coming and tramping on the village*).

Follow-up
Independent Group Activity Work

This book is accompanied by two photocopy masters, one with a reading focus, and one with a writing focus, which support the teaching objectives of this book. The photocopy masters can be found in the Planning and Assessment Guide.

PCM F5.1 (*reading*)

PCM F5.2 (*writing*)

You may also like to invite the children to read the story again during their independent reading (either at school or at home).

Writing

Guided writing: Identify with the children the connective phrases and words which form the narrative (e.g. *One night, when, then,* etc) and use these in their own stories.

Extended writing: Write a play based on the story.

Assessment Points

Assess that the children have learnt the main teaching points of the book by checking that they can:

- identify why certain things happen
- identify why characters change through the story (e.g. the elves' changing perception of Korka).